The Wonderful World of Model Trains

A Beginner's Guide to Building Your Own Model Railways and Creating Stunning Sceneries & Layouts

David B. Brokaw

The Wonderful World of Model Trains

Publisher: Living Plus Healthy Publishing

ISBN-13: 978-1496158918

ISBN-10: 1496158911

Disclaimer

The Publisher has strived to be as accurate and complete as possible in the creation of this book. While all attempts have been made to verify information provided in this publication, the Publisher assumes no responsibility for errors, omissions, or contrary interpretation of the subject matter herein. Any perceived slights of specific persons, peoples, or organizations are unintentional.

This book is not intended for use as a source of legal, business, accounting or financial advice. All readers are advised to seek services of competent professionals in the legal, business, accounting, and finance fields.

The information in this book is not intended or implied to be a substitute for professional medical advice, diagnosis or treatment. All content contained in this book is for general information purposes only. Always consult your healthcare provider before carrying on any health program.

Table of Contents

Introduction

Model railroading used to be a very popular hobby in the "old days" before the invention of modern technologies that are now preferred by many for entertainment these days. Rarely are model trains even mentioned as a possible hobby to enjoy in today's culture. The hobby faded out gradually through the years as more and more technological advancements and inventions took over their popularity in entertainment priorities.

Other than those who are "accidental" railroad enthusiasts because of close family members who love model railroading, knowledge of model railroads and what they can offer today is virtually unknown to younger generations. While that is regrettable, it can also be beneficial for young and old alike by infecting (or re-infecting) them with the model train "bug" that seems to be a "new" discovery to the young.

Trains can hold the interest of younger generations as well as older ones partly because the railroad technologies have also advanced with the culture and are beginning to gain more and more value as educational entertainment that offers a lot of fun and learning to railroaders of any age. Sometimes children will place more value on knowledge that seems like a new discovery to them.

We tend to dismiss any hobbies or entertainment that our ancestors enjoyed as ones with little value in reality today in light of our technological advances. Returning to hobbies of old can seem like a regression back to times where "they didn't know any better" and to hobbies that were "endured" because there was nothing better available. Progression can be valued too highly in every generation and can cause us to "throw out the baby with the bath water".

There are many areas in our culture today that could enjoy various benefits offered through enjoying the hobby of model railroads and it is rewarding to help people discover for themselves just how much fun and educational value railroads have to offer.

Now, let's discover those benefits together.

Chapter 1: Why Model Railroading?

Family Reasons

Bonding Tool

Not only is model railroading a unique hobby to enjoy with the youth of the home, their friends, and your friends, it is just as valuable as a bonding tool between the older generations and younger – especially grandparents or elderly family and friends who play similar roles in the lives of your children.

Sometimes it can be difficult to find common ground between the old and the young that is entertaining enough for both generations to enjoy and want more of. It is status quo in our technological age for the youth in families to be much more knowledgeable and perhaps even a bit arrogant about computers, cell phones, and all the electronics that might be unfamiliar and/or uncomfortable for older generations.

Children are often seen teaching their grandparents how to operate a computer, voice messaging on cell phones, and MP3 players, etc. Train sets can be a unique "leveler" that allows both generations to be more knowledgeable than the other in some areas which can be great for helping both understand the valuable strengths each can offer as they work together with a model railroad.

The young might better understand the technological advancements that are available now for railroading involving technology that did not exist for earlier generations. But the knowledge available through life experience and wisdom coupled with the "know-how" to enjoy model railroads to the utmost with more over-all knowledge belongs to older generations who might have been playing with these railroad systems for more than 50 years or so.

Building a railroad model together will cause the young to respect the knowledge and experience of their elders and perhaps be surprised at the fun that can be enjoyed with them. And the elders just might be appreciative and proud of all intelligence of the young and how easy technology is for them to master.

The level of successful enjoyment of the model-railroading hobby in terms of generational bonding time is best when everyone respects each other's strength while being patient with each other's weaknesses. Either way – in a world of chaos where the familiar age-old struggle of trying to forge connections between generations is common, model railroads might give you a perfect bonding tool from a direction that neither generation might be expecting.

Family Night

Since railroading might be good fit to build relationships between the older generation and the younger, it is also easily adaptable for enjoyment during family time that involves multiple generations from our parents, to us as parents, and to the children we are raising.

Grandparents might have more time to enjoy railroading with their grandchildren who also might have more time available when compared to the middle generation responsible for the needs of the young and the old of the family. But the good news is that railroading lends itself well to entertain whoever is around during any given family time and doesn't require the presence of anyone specially in order to enjoy the hobby during family times together.

A frequent disagreement or conflict between parents and children is the amount of time spent playing video games and watching televisions. Model railroading can address this easily as middle ground because it is both educational and entertaining. It is a healthy activity and a good way to encourage your children to play that is productive and mentally stimulating at the same time.

Learning Tool

The educational value that can be found in building model railways is far greater than might seem possible when first considering the topic. Oh, sure – railroad knowledge is great for educational lessons in engineering, mechanics, or math but it goes far beyond that in both direct and indirect education.

The educational concepts that can be taught through building railroading are many, and are not limited to the education of children. Anyone at any age who enjoys learning will enjoy the educational perspective available with railroading – here are just a few of the ways model railroads can be educational for any and all who participate in the activity.

History Lessons

Model trains are a great tool to use for teaching historical facts of the railroading era along with the accomplishments our ancestors made through railroad discoveries and construction.

Our railroad history through the years is an impressive and thought-provoking aspect of the past including: what railroads offered to cattle ranchers, what cultural or environmental issues were created because of the railroad expansions, how railroad travel affected how long it took to get from one end of the country to the other, etc.

The model-railroading hobby can also teach about the advancements of technology through the years as it relates to trains and the mechanics of operating a railroad successfully. The history of steam engines and coal burners can be learned by building or discussing the history of trains.

The history of train robberies derailments during the Wild West days can be learned by pointing out areas along your railroad that would be vulnerable for outlaws seeking to rob the train or even choosing that scenario as a theme for the model if wanted.

Native American history can also be taught both in ways their culture was negatively and positively affected through railroads, and also some of the ways that influenced the attacks Indians carried out by ambushing trains or causing derailments. There are many ways railroads have influenced history and what better time to learn then when building a rail-roading.

Scientific Lessons

Model trains also have value from a scientific viewpoint making the hobby a great source for various projects that both children and adults can enjoy such as scientific experiments, school assignments, science competition, mathematical equations, physic properties and concepts, and engineering feats, etc.

Building a railroading system can offer some fun ways to give children a deeper understanding with some complex topics that might be briefly touched on in school like building to scale, the engineering details for building a train bridge over a canyon, mechanical operations involved with running the trains, and the law of gravity, etc., just to name a few.

Even if you decide railroading is "just for fun" for yourself and/or your family, education and learning are still accomplished without being obvious and can be another tool that might help young people realize just how much fun education can be. Not only that, railroads also have great potential for awakening curiosity and feeding that thirst for knowledge and problem solving both through enjoying the railroading hobby presently while also recognizing the ingenious discoveries and engineering feats previous generations gifted to all coming behind them.

Health Benefits

Can there really be health benefits to enjoying railroading as a hobby? Most definitely! – more than you would probably imagine. We have already discussed how it can be beneficial to the mental health of the elderly, and beneficial to the educational health of the developing minds of young people, but railroading can have more direct impacts on various other health issues as well that might surprise you.

Physical Rehab

Model railroading can be an excellent tool for use during various kinds of physical rehab from illness, injuries, or surgery. Whether one is working on overcoming brain trauma to recovering from a badly mangled hand or anything in between, railroading gives an enjoyable but challenging workout in ways that make recovery a little more pleasant than traditional rehab techniques.

The various items in a railroad set are great for working out damaged hands and fingers because the sizes of the items are different offering a wide level of necessary challenges from the simple, such as setting a train car securely on the tracks, to the more complex, such as hooking up the little couplings that connect the trains or the various switches needing manipulated to run the set. Model railroads can bring a measure of enjoyment to grueling rehab sessions that usually have very little "fun" to offer during recovery.

Brain Damage Treatment

Brain damage can be addressed with a rail-roading system in terms of memory among other things. The names for the different pieces and equipment can be as simple as necessary or as difficult as need be in order to challenge memory to perform better. It can also be helpful when trying to re-train the mind/body connection between the brain and the hands by getting hand movements to cooperate with brain commands. Even thinking through the decisions of which piece is the next to purchase and planning out the set on paper before purchase is a great mental exercise for those trying to regain brain function after damage.

Distraction from Various Limitations

Railroading can offer a simple and/or complex source of enjoyment and distraction when dealing with any kind of long-term disease or chronic illness that forces varying degrees of physical activity limitations and/or mental stimulation limitations. Perhaps a child needs to be still for 2 hours after the latest chemo or IV treatment – running a railroad set from the tableside or bedside can create enough distraction giving the child some enjoyment while enduring whatever physical challenges he is facing.

Maybe railroading would be just the thing needed to ease the depression of a middle-aged man recovering from open-heart surgery and the limitations that has placed on his life whether temporary or long-term. Model railroads might be just "what the doctor ordered" for entertainment when physical and mental stimulations have to be carefully limited in order to keep heart rates down, etc.

Most of us as adults have a part of us that has never grown up and would enjoy playing with toys. Railroading is a "toy" that is better accepted as an adult hobby than playing with dolls or toy soldiers or the like similar to what you used to enjoy when actually still a child.

The pleasure from all the different aspects and development of a model railroad system might be able to help someone whose life has been permanently changed through illness or accident and offer a way relax and re-evaluate life while organizing and arranging a train set.

Coping Skill

Not only can railroading be significantly useful when recovering from or dealing with the limitations resulting from physical illness and injury, it can also be a positive coping skill to use when dealing with mental illness itself regardless of the cause. It can help a season of depression induced by surgeries and new limitations such as the heart surgery mentioned above, but it can also be a great, out-of-the-box solution for some of those who are dealing with chronic mental illness such as schizophrenia, obsessive-compulsive disorder, bipolar disorder, etc., etc.

Whether used as a comfort skill when stress levels are too high or used to challenge repetitive behaviors that are unhealthy to anything in between, railroading is a good direction to consider researching and jumping into if you or someone you love is struggling with mental illness and needs something that will add to the quality of life.

Just Plain Fun!

Last but not least, choosing railroading for a hobby is just plain fun! Some may have the most fun planning the layout and building it piece by piece just right from their own unique perspective. Others have the most fun watching loved ones enjoy playing with their railroad. And yet others find the most fun in the pleasure and speed of running trains around the track in your own personally created layout.

There are many ways to enjoy building and playing with a railroad, and you have probably realized the ways you can personally enjoy model railroads, so now, let's look at the facts, information, and choices necessary to turn this fun hobby into reality in your life!

Chapter 2: Understanding the Basics

Scale & Gauge Definitions

You will hear the word "scale" often when building a model railroad so it is important you understand that "scale" is a measurement (or ratio) of the size differences between a real railroad, and a model railroad.

In case you do not remember how ratio numbers translate, consider the ratio of a locomotive train car. Say the scale is 1:24 – mentally consider an image of a full-size locomotive in your mind and then create a grid dividing it into 24 equal parts. Consider just one of those 24 parts – your model-sized locomotive, a tiny version of the real thing, would be only as big as one of those 24 grid pieces you divided the real train into in your mind's eye.

That process makes the ratio of this model locomotive to a real locomotive be 1:24 – the mini locomotive is as small as just one of the divided portions of the real one thus having the ratio of 1:24.

While there are quite a few different scale ratios or sizes available to use while building a railroad, the main ones (and the most popular) are the G scale, HO scale, N scale, O scale, and S scale.

G Scale

The G scale is mainly used for railroad that will be built and run outside in a garden-type setting. Ratios vary a bit in the G scale and can range from 1:19 to 1:29. The gauge used in most railways of the G scale is 45 mm (see gauge definition below).

HO Scale

The HO scale is a bit smaller than the G scale with a ration of 1:87 with rail gauge between 6.5 mm and 16.5 mm depending on which version of the HO scales. It is the scale size used most commonly by railroading enthusiasts so there are many options for railroad pieces with the HO scale then are available with the other scales. This is also the size of model trains that older people remember from the past as the model train craze of the 70's used the HO scale size for the most part.

N Scale

The N scale is another popular scale with a ratio ranging from 1:148 to 1:160 with a gauge of 9 mm. It is sometimes preferred over the HO scale because it is so much smaller and will take less space than an HO railway. Building a N Scale train system can be even more elaborate with more room available for longer tracks, etc.

S Scale

The S scale uses a ratio of 1:64 with its standard gauge of 22.42 mm, and is one of the first scales created in model railroading beginning in 1896. One of its better features is the selection of pieces and products available that are high quality and detailed making the S scale a great choice when interested in building a well-rounded rail system with all the accessories and aesthetic decorations possible.

O Scale

The ratio of the O scale varies according to the different standards a country has ranging from 1:43 in England, 1:45 in the main parts of Europe, and 1:48 in the United States with a common gauge to all round 31.75 mm. This size is very popular for children's toy train sets and was the most popular size in the States until the 1960's because it was so cheap and durable. The Great Depression and its economic impact required cheaper options were needed instead of the other more detailed scales that were more realistic but also more expensive. When other scale sizes regained popularity as the economy improved, sales of the O scale dropped. However, during the 1990's manufacturers of railroading supplies began to focus on making their O scale items more realistic so it is again becoming quite popular although not yet as much as the HO or N scales.

Gauge

One of the technicalities of railroading that can be confusing is the gauge properties. Quite often railroading literature or information will use the words "scale" and "gauge" interchangeably implying they are the same thing, but technically they are not.

It is important to know that gauge only refers to the distance between the two rails of a track while scale is in reference to the size of the entire rail system. In other words, gauges fit within the definitions included in scale descriptions so can be used interchangeably as long as you understand that gauge measurements are specifics under the umbrella of the defined scale.

Most scales have a gauge or range of gauges it must have in order to meet the standards set for the scale.

National Model Railroaders Association Information

History

The first documented model railroad was built in a park of the Nymphenberg Castle grounds in Germany by Josef von Baader in order to promote a real railway project he had in mind. He hoped to catch the interest of the King and it worked – the real railroad project based on Baader's model was completed in 1835. That was the start of what was to become a favorite hobby of entertainment by old and young, rich and poor all around the world.

Until the 1930's, all model railroad train cars and parts were as different as the manufacturers wanted them to be with very little cooperation or communication between manufactures. This disallowed for making the parts interchangeable when purchased by from different manufacturing sources.

Model railroaders found that one manufacture's trains didn't necessarily work with a different manufacturer's tracks, etc. There was no conformity of parts or sizes – not from the smallest couplers combining train cars to the largest track they ran on.

But in 1935, the National Model Railroaders Association (NMRA) was created during a meeting between railroaders and manufacturers and they began to develop universal standard guidelines in order resolve the chaos and confusion that marked the hobby at the time.

NMRA Standards

The standard guidelines were established by the National Model Railroad Association in 1936 and have changed very little since then. Obviously, the NMRA put a lot of time and effort into their decisions that have remained strong from 1936 until now without a need for major changes in between.

Of course they have been adjusted and expanded in order to keep up with changing technologies, etc., but the foundational standards remain the same. In fact, the effectiveness of those standards created an organized hobby that could then use those standards to advance model railroading to the system we have today. According to their official website:

"NMRA STANDARDS provide the primary basis upon which interchange between equipment and various North American scale model railroads is founded. Under this requirement NMRA STANDARDS include only those factors that are considered vital to such Interchange. For less critical matters see the NMRA RECOMMENDED PRACTICES."

In plain English, the NMRA standards set the numerical values and boundaries for each piece and size of the various scales with measurements that are constant and universal for each scale. Manufactures must adhere to the guidelines if they want to claim membership with the NMRA and the benefits to their sales it provides.

These standards are highly respected by model railroaders and when purchasing products for railroading, seeing the seal of the NMRA membership on product packaging and paperwork allows them to know they are buying from a reputable manufacturer and are safe to trust their purchases will fit their own railroad as promised.

NMRA Recommended Practices

Not only has the NMRA set standards that have greatly benefitted the hobby of railroading, they also have recommendations for railroading that use the NMRA standards and are the results of actual testing done using the technical details mandated by NMRA standards. Manufacturers do not get the official NMRA seal of approval without their information being tested and proven as accurate. In some ways, these recommended practices can be even more valuable for the novice railroader saving them time and frustration of having to test measurements themselves to see if they work or not.

Chapter 3: Preliminary Plans

Now that you know just how much fun model railroading can be, and you understand some of its terminologies including scale, gauge, and standards, it is now time to actually start the process of building your model railroad system.

The first step in the building process is determining the layout of your benchwork. Benchwork is simply a term for the platform structure your entire railroad system will sit on. There are different aspects of the benchwork that would work best if adapted to various details of the unique track plan for your train set.

At this point you need to have a general plan in mind of how you want your system to be laid out. It is extremely helpful to have a rough sketch of your system plans in order to start building the benchwork. It might also be beneficial to loosely lay out train tracks on the floor in order to get a general idea of the size of benchwork you need and whether or not it will fit in the space you have available.

Track Plan

There are a few details that you need to decide in order to customize your benchwork to fit the system you have planned. It is much easier (not to mention less frustrating) to plan the foundational benchwork first and then build the train system In order to limit the risks of discovering halfway through your model train set up that your benchwork is too small.

You still may discover that there are changes you would like to make during and after you have completed construction, and that's okay. But working from a plan at first will cut down on the confusion and lessen how many changes you will need to accommodate later.

Space

When designing your own personalized train system, you first must decide and measure how much space is available to dedicate to your train system. Whether it is an entire room or just part of one, you must have those measurements to start with in order to design your system efficiently.

Once you know how much room you have to work with and you have your general trackplan mentioned above, you can then begin to organize and build your benchwork. The general size of the area for your train system should be established by now so it is time to make decisions as to how you are going to best use that dedicated space.

Access

You may have found that you have a 7 feet by 10 feet space overall to build your benchwork for example, but that does not mean you start designing your train stage on a 7x9 platform. That would leave much of your system unreachable and create great frustration. It is best if you arrange your space and benchwork in order to reach all parts of your system. This can be done by having an aisle all the way around your system, or it can also be done by have a "hole" in the very middle of your platform with a crawlspace below it in order to reach that hole and "pop" up in the middle of your railroad.

Whichever method you decide to utilize, each and every aspect of your system should be within arm's reach from one point or another if at all possible. What if you don't design it that way? Well, consider having your stage to be that 7x9 platform mentioned above that has to fit into a 7x10 space in general.

If you put the 7x9 platform into a 7x10 space, logically, 3 sides would be flush up again the walls or whatever obstacles making the 7x10 feet boundaries necessary. If you have 3 sides of your system up against the walls, most derailments or adjustments necessary will be a bit stressful to care for when your arms are not long enough to reach all the back to the farthest corners when needed.

If you created a "pop-up" hole in the center of that platform, you would then be able to crawl under it, pop through the hole, and be able to reach all 4 corners of your system from that hole. Or, you could build a smaller benchwork in the space available making sure there is enough room for you to maneuver around the benchwork on all sides enabling you to have the access necessary in order to make changes or fix problems.

If you have the space to do so, the most efficient and least frustrating benchwork will make sure there is plenty of walking space aisles around all four sides of the benchwork which will have a lot to do with whether model railroading will be enjoyed, or if it will be more stressful than fun because you have to struggle to reach the farthest areas of your railroad.

Track Configuration

Depending on your track plan, the configuration of the tracks can be as simple as a single loop track running continuously in a circle or as complicated as multiple staging yards that are capable of receiving and sending several trains in different directions on more than one level.

Levels

When you are new and inexperienced with model trains, it would probably be best to limit your system to a single level that can be added to later on down the road as you get the hang of it and determine whether this is going to be a long-term hobby or just a passing fancy.

Being able to add levels to your train set in the future if desired makes railroading possibilities more interesting to some in knowing there are always more things to add and expand your railroad in almost limitless directions so there will never be an end to the fun of model railroads.

Loop-to-Loop Tracks

When a track is laid to run in a continuous circle or oval from beginning to end it is said to be loop-to-loop. This means that the tracks only allow the train to go in one direction and in order to get from one end of the track to the other, it has to run the circle around always in the same direction. In this general scenario, the "staging yard" is where you add or remove train cars and engines from the tracks and they both arrive and depart from that staging yard in the same direction.

Point-to-Loop Tracks

In a point-to-loop track layout, the points are staging yards that can run a train onto the track at any time but the train then needs to be added back to the mainline in the same direction that any other trains on the system are running. When a train arrives at a staging yard point in this case, the train itself needs to be turned around in order to re-enter that track layout.

This can add a level of complication that can either be frustrating and limiting to your fun, OR there are ways to solve this situation and others within your layout which is some of what makes model railroads so entertaining with the problem solving aspects that are very satisfying when you figure out the answer.

In this case, one way to fix the problem of having to turn the train around manually so it can run back on the track, is by adding an extra loop to your staging area that you then send the train through allowing it to reverse and go back instead of having to flip the train around yourself.

Loop and Point Combinations

Of course like most other complex and thereby enjoyable hobbies, railroad systems can be customized and modified to personal preferences. The track configuration is one of the most helpful tools to use in building the system you have in mind. Your own unique track configuration can include multiple scenarios that use both loop and point track layouts to build your system the way you want it to be built.

Scenic Environment

Now that the foundational elements are decided, it is time to settle on the overall look for your system. In other words, what scenario do you want your model to replicate and how it will fit into the plan you have set for benchwork and layout.

Historical

You could build a replication of railroading to model the first railroad line that was built East to West. You can run it through the mountains and valleys of the rural areas in the West with Indians and buffalo, etc. in the background, or model an area that was notorious for bank robbers and Indians to ambush using canyons and blind curves.

Or maybe build a model train going through a town in the Wild West, or a model to illustrate what it looked like through the construction phases of adding one track at a time through various challenges, or a railroad model of it worked when cattle first started getting shipped via rail with trail drives to the nearest depot, etc. – just to name a few theme ideas.

American history and how it relates to railroading has many options to choose from that could be a lot of fun to re-create, but would require a plan first in order to make sure your benchwork has room for the elements you want to create.

Modern

You may prefer to build a modern railroad that exemplifies the technological advances that have occurred through the years in railroading. Maybe you want your trains to run through a miniature industrial area with industry buildings and business' such as coal and fuel transportation, chemical or milk distribution, or multitudes of other ways current railroads are used for.

Do you want your trains to be passenger trains with staging yards/depots for arrival and departures? Or maybe a model of nuclear, biohazard chemicals, military transportation needs, etc.? What about modern day cattle, food, and/or crop transportation, etc.? Just as there are many ideas for your system from a historical perspective, there are also many options for creating a modern railroad replica as well.

No matter what theme you decide on for your unique and personalized model, you must determine the space it will require in order to know build an appropriate benchwork that will allow you to create the system you have envisioned.

System Mobility

When you are planning the benchwork (as well as the rest of the system) you need to consider what your goals are both in terms of your model railroad as well as your life in general. If you need your system to be portable for whatever reason, that needs to be a consideration as you decide all the elements involved but especially while designing and building your benchwork.

Do you plan on moving your system to school or other informational and/or competitive activities and events? What about moving? Is relocation to a new home or city a possibility in the near future? Knowing whether you are planning to transport your system anywhere, and how often you may do so will decide some of the more technical elements of building the benchwork for you.

Portable

It is fairly simple to build your system in a way that will make it easy to transport if that is your goal, and you incorporate that factor with your track plan and benchwork. For example, the platform can be built with hinges that allow it to fold up. The scenery can be divided into sections easy to take apart and designed to fit into whatever totes or boxes you want to use to protect your handiwork while moving it from point A to point B and back again.

Immobile

On the flip side, you may want to make sure your railroad is NOT portable for various reasons. You may be asked but they can't expect you to show your system at your grandchild's show-&- tell at school, or loaned as decoration for some family event or another if it is built in a way that makes it virtually impossible to remove from your home without destroying a good portion of the set-up or without taking ridiculous amounts of time for transport.

Ensuring your railroad is as least portable as possible also lessens the risks of it being stolen if your house gets burglarized or someone decides to take possession without permission for whatever reason. If you would enjoy taking it for a show-&-tell at school, or sharing the fun and novelty at an event, then you would prefer it to be easily transported and can build it accordingly. But if you would rather keep your system home and secure, safe and sound, limiting its portability will help support that preference.

Other Considerations

The last thing you need to consider before you begin building the actual framework is the room area where you are planning to build and keep your railroad. Are there renovations you would like to do within the space while it is still empty? Do you want to put a fresh coat of paint on the walls knowing it would be easier to do so before your system is built and in the way?

What about the flooring – need new carpeting or hardwood floors put in first? How is the lighting in the area – do you need to install a ceiling fan and light? It is a lot more fun and relaxing to enjoy your model railroad yourself and enjoy sharing or showing it off to others if the area around it is clean, well-lit, with moderate temperatures, and visually attractive.

Building the Benchwork

Hardware Supply Options

You've thought it through and have planned your benchwork with decisions according to personal preferences for various options, and you have created an open, inviting area for your railroad. All that's left before starting the actual construction phase is the task of gathering building tools and the supplies your particular benchwork plan requires. But you might want to consider an alternative to building your own benchwork by enlisting the help of carpenters, etc. that are in your life, especially if you are new to model railroading or construction techniques, or if you are not sure you will enjoy it enough for it to be a long-term hobby.

Positioning

Whether you build your own staging platform or benchwork, or adapt various furniture or hardware items for your benchwork instead, there are several things you need to keep in mind that will limit some frustrations further down the road.

We have already talked about making sure you are able to access all areas of the system whether by an adequate aisle all the way around the benchwork, or through a hole in the center of the layout. Those details will be dictated by the space available to use compared with the specifics of your track plan.

You also need to think about where the wiring for your system is going to wind up, if your platform is reinforced enough to withstand the weight of your system, where the lighting is or isn't going to be, the storage for various train accessories not in use all the time, whether you plan to sit or stand when running your trains, etc., etc.

Visual Level

Ideally, your model should be built some-where between eye level and waist level. Vis-ually, it is best to have the model at average eye level, but that isn't always best for body mechanics if you need to be able to build and adjust your railroad without having to keep your arms elevated for the extended periods of time necessary for model railroading. Since a model railroad is visually at its best at eye level, but physically best around waist level, compromise is key in deciding the height of your system. Somewhere between eye level and waist level is a height that will work suffi-ciently for both needs.

Height & Grid Work

It is best if there is storage and/or working space below the tabletop of the benchwork specifically for the many wires and electrical system used for your train among other things. Not only should this area be able to somewhat organize the wires and keep them out of the way, it also needs to allow for easy access of the same wiring as needed. The height of the platform will also aid in this as the higher it is, the easier it will be to work with the wiring underneath.

It works great if there is a type of screen or grid work attached to the underside of the benchwork top that allows the wiring to only be visible from underneath while keeping it up off the floor and potential damage it could incur there. A grid work will also allow wiring to be easily secured with twist ties or zip ties that can keep it all neatly in place where it belongs lessening the opportunities for creating a jumbled, tangled mess of wires.

Storage Space

Having storage space under your benchwork goes a long way in simplifying the hobby of railroading both for keeping all your tools and various working items together and also as a simple way to easily find your train supplies in a central location for any accessories not used in the everyday operation of your railroad. You can use storage spaces under the benchwork by storing train paraphernalia in various sized storage totes that will fit in the space, or you can also place simple shelving or cubbyholes to organize the items making them easier to see quickly and find whatever you are looking for.

If you are repurposing a piece of furniture for your benchwork, it might already have doors built in that can hide the storage area, but if not, or if you are building your own, consider what would work best for you and your system. It is better to be able to close doors or draw curtains that will keep the clutter and wiring out of sight beneath the benchwork if possible. Not only will you enjoy running your system without the cluttered distractions, but it will also be more enjoyable to have that hidden when showing it off to others interested in seeing it and playing with it.

Miscellaneous Options

There are various options for benchwork available depending on how much money you want to spend, how much construction knowledge you have, and how much time you want to invest, etc. These options range from:

- using a piece of furniture you already have and adapting it as much as possible to meet your layout needs,

- using an average-sized wood door securely screwed into a couple of wooden sawhorses,
- building your own benchwork following purchased plans or through your own calculations,
- ordering custom-cut lumber from your nearest hardware store or lumberyard,
- purchasing a building kit that has all the hardware and pre-cut lumber included,
- hiring a professional builder to build the exact plans you have envisioned,
- or even purchasing a pre-fabricated benchwork made specifically for model railroads that requires little assembly, but neither does it allow for any custom sizes or detail changes.

How you go about creating the benchwork for your system is up to you and how much you would enjoy (or not) the various aspects of constructing the foundation necessary for your model before you can begin to build or set up the actual railroad itself.

Chapter 4: Tracks & Wiring

Track Designs

There are some basic details for track designs that you need to know in order to have the knowledge necessary to create your own track plan in ways that you prefer while also managing some of the specifics that could become frustrating if they are not addressed in your track plan. Whether you have a simple track layout of a single oval on one layer or you want to build a complex train system with several layers and other intricate design details, you need to know the important things to keep in mind while deciding what your layout will include and what it won't.

Basic Continuous Running Designs (also known as loop to loop)

The following basic designs for track layouts will work well alone or in various combinations depending on how much space you have for the railroad system and how many levels you are planning to include. These designs can be stretched out, multi-layered, or reduced to develop your own unique track plan. Keep in mind that you don't have to start out with intricate track designs because you can and probably will change and add to your design as you go along which is part of what makes model railroading fun!

- **Simple Oval** – The simple oval is just that…a simple oval that can be adjusted into more or less a circle or oval – which ever you prefer. This is usually what most model railroads start with and then the layout is expanded to add different aspects according to preference and space.

- **Figure Eight** – The figure eight track design is…yes…a figure eight! Go figure! This simple lay out calls for a cross-over of sorts in the middle that generally requires a way for the tracks to cross over the top of each other such as a tunnel for the lower half that allows the upper half to crossover, or the upper half can be on a bridge giving the lower level the space to go under the bridge.

- **Twice Around** – The twice around is merely two ovals intertwined with 3-4 crossover points between them. Each crossover point has to be configured in a way that allows for continuous run of the train in similar ways to the figure eight needs in a crossover configuration.

- **Dogbone** – The dogbone track design looks more like a pair of binoculars in shape of the layout at least, and gives an interesting element to your design where the two sides of the track come close to meeting each other in the middle while leaving enough space for trains to pass side by side without touching. This is a design that would work well if you want to incorporate a mountain and valley – one side of the track would run through the valley at the bottom of the mountain while the other side would run on the top or side of the mountain.

- **Folded Dogbone** – The folded dogbone is the most complex of the basic designs and can be adjusted in multiple ways to allow for many different details you might want to build. If thinking of this design as a pair of binoculars like the basic dogbone design, it would call for a stretch of the mid-piece of the binoculars (kind of like pulling taffy) then one end or the other is flipped and folded back to make both sides of the "binocular" to both be on one side as a mirror image of each other. You have all sorts of possibilities for crossovers, valley, mountains, side-by-sides, etc. when using this design.

Configuration Options

- **Easements** – Easements are sections of track headed into and/or coming out of curves that allow the curve radius to be slower and easier to navigate. If you think of easements as track sections that allow a train to "ease into curves", you are right. While not necessarily a requirement for your system, easements lessen the chance of derailments on the curves from having a turn that is too sharp. Easements will also model real railroads that seek to avoid sharp turning that results in a jolt to any passengers on board or to fragile freight being transported.

Just like we do not care for fast and sharp turns while driving cars that cause a jerking of the body and neck, train passengers are likewise unhappy with sharp curves and including easements should resolve the issue. Easements start the train curving sooner than it would happen without them which in turn gives a more gradual turning option.

Easements won't require more space in the overall layout but any surrounding scenery or accessories might need adjusted to make room for that more gradual turn. For example, you might have a grove of trees on the inside of a curve that will need to be re-arranged with some of the trees going on the outside of the track instead allowing the curved track to fit in that area.

Utilizing easements is also more visually attractive when watching a train run through the railroad layout. Most people will not enjoy watching a train jerk and turn hard at a curve like it is part of an amusement park ride. Technically, model railroads are simply a smaller version of the real thing and very rarely will a real train layout hit sharp curves like that. Not only does it risk a derailment, but it is unnecessary wear and tear on the engine and cars, especially the coupling connections between them.

- **Turn Around Choices** – There are different track options available that will allow you to turn your train around while still on the tracks without having to physically pick up the train off the tracks and turn it around. These track sections are called turntables or turnouts.

If left out, this will be a part of your railroad system that will sooner or later be very frustrating and impact how much you enjoy running your train if you had to pick it up to turn it around. Again, this is modeling a real railroad and clearly, physically picking up a train and turning it around doesn't happen in real life with the exception of a repair yard where different engines and cars might be rearranged using a crane while being built or repaired.

Turnouts do not have to be used all the time if you install them in your layout as the switches installed along with them can be left alone if no changes in direction are desired at any given time. Wyes and reversing loops add more intricate options that will in turn add more entertainment value to your model railroad.

- **Wyes** – Wyes are another term in model railroading that is very self-descriptive. These sections of track are in the shape of the letter "y". Wyes will direct your train right or left allowing it to go in different directions, but not straight ahead.

- **Reversing Tracks** – Reversing tracks do just that...reverse a train back onto the same track going in the opposite direction. These loops can be included anywhere that you might want to have the option of turning your train to run back in the direction it was coming from.

Additional Train Movement Options

- **Whole Train Maneuvering** – Having the ability to move and rearrange entire trains or single locomotives and cars in multiple ways while running your system is another element that adds to the enjoyment of the model-railroading hobby. If you plan to run several trains on your system at the same time, use of runarounds or passing siding track sections allow you to pull entire trains off the main track either to wait for a faster train to pass, or to avoid blocking the main line by being stationary for any length of time.

- **Single Train Re-Configuring** – Not only will you need to be able to move multiple trains the entire train with its locomotives and cars at the same time, you also need to be able to rearrange the engines and cars within individual trains. The runaround and passing siding track arrangements work with rearranging single trains as well – especially if you are changing cars or engines from one train to another. You can utilize these sections to move a locomotive from the front of a train to the back or various rearrangements of the cars connected.

- **Runaround** – A runaround section of track is very handy to have available when you are running multiple trains on your system. These can be utilized to avoid blocking the "main lane" of a railroad by allowing one train to pull off to the side of the main track in order to unload freight or passengers, allow for a faster train to pass without causing a traffic jam of sorts by blocking the main track, or for rearranging the individual cars connected within a train. This is quite similar to common driving procedures where cars are supposed to pull off to the shoulder of the highway if needing to stop for any reason in order to not block the road for those coming along behind.

- **Passing Siding** – Passing sidings are similar to runarounds except they are generally used just as "passing" lanes of sorts without stopping for an extended period of time like is necessary for unloading freight and passengers. Passing siding can be "conventional" or "lapped". Conventional siding adds a turnout section to just one side of the main line where lapped siding allows turnouts on either side of the mainline running.

- **Ladder** – In model railroading terms, a ladder is a section of track that belongs in a train yard to help sort and re-configure trains as needed. In essence, it is a straight piece of track that is connected to mainline on each end, but also has several dead end track sections that will allow cars to be lined up and connected to the train that is waiting on the straight piece connected to the mainline.

- **Spur** – Spurs are short branches of track that splice off the mainline for multiple uses necessary to run various services such as passenger and freight, or when using trains with import and export of any industrial part of your entire system. If you are building a complex system or when you start adding on to your basic system, spurs can be installed with each building in the layout in order to leave or rearrange cars and locomotives as needed by the various components such as passenger trains, stock freighting, repairs yards, coal or chemical depots, etc. Spurs simply allow cars or even entire trains to pull off the main track in order to not hold up the line for any trains coming along.

Those are the generalized and basic elements of track layout options available to consider when determining your own individual railroad layout that can be as unique as you want it to be. Any component or aspect of railroading that you want to be a part of your own system can be included, and the above layout options give some idea of how a railroad can be configured to your own preferences.

How To Lay Tracks

Once you have considered the options available for personalizing your model rail system, you are able to decide on your layout plans which should be initially created on paper using a pencil and preferably graph paper that will allow you to be more specific in the planning stage. The more accurately detailed your plans are, the less work and frustration potential you'll have while actually building the track system.

Assuming you have completed your layout plans (in pencil of course as more than likely there will be changes as you go along), the steps necessary to do the actual laying of your tracks is surprisingly simple for the most part especially when following a well thought out plan. This is probably when your personal model railroad enjoyment will go from "interesting" to "exciting" as you begin to see your vision come together right underneath your own hands!

Remember...your track plans were not drawn with pencil just for the fun of it. Always keep in mind one of the important tenets of model railroading that contributes greatly to its entertainment value is that plans can always change as you go along and probably will...especially if you are new to the hobby. So accept a big eraser as your building partner while you create the vision of your model train system.

Step 1

Having your written plans, necessary track sections, and clear benchwork within reach, the first step in building your trackplan is laying out the tracks loosely following the plans you created. No need to physically connect tracks sections or attach them to the benchwork at this time.

The reasons for this are two-fold. First, it allows you to evaluate whether or not the trackplans you created are realistically possible or not and if there are changes you need to make in order to fit the trackplan to the benchwork space.

Second, the reason for loosely laying out the tracks is to see what adjustments you might prefer now that you can see it laying in front of you in 3-D. Some details are not no-ticeably out of place or imbalanced when on paper, but once the plan is laid out physically, you might see areas that need rearranging in order to be as visually attractive as possible.

Step 2

Once you see the rough layout and make whatever changes you want or need to, the focus then switches to the turnouts that are part of your plan. The turnouts (as described above) are the sections of track that direct the train off the main track line for numerous rea-sons. In order to cause the train to turn off the main track, you need to utilize a mechanism called a "switch" that diverts the tracks and thus the train into various turnouts and off the main line.

Switches are the single most necessary part of your railroad layout if you have anything other than just a single train loop as they are what allow you to direct the running of your trains in whatever manner desired. The switches are used sporadically as needed and when not engaged, they just go "silent" and do not influence the directions trains are run-ning.

When building turnouts and switches you can either have manual switches that you have to throw yourself in order to engage and send the train in the direction you want it to go, or you can have the switches be controlled via a remote control. If planning on using a remote to throw the switches, then where you actually install the turnouts and corresponding switches doesn't matter much. But if you are planning on throwing the switches manually, you need to make sure that all the switches are within reach as you are laying down your tracks.

You can also use a mixture of both manual and remote switches configured however works best to fit with your plan and bench-work access. Using both methods might be more beneficial if there are areas of the system that are either hard to reach or nigh to impossible to reach at arm's length. Having turnouts and switches in difficult-to-reach sections of your railroad managed with a remote control may help limit the frustrations of trying to get to a switch that isn't near enough to do so easily. Other than that type of scenario, whether you use manual switches, remote controlled ones, or a combination of both is simply a matter of preference for the most part.

The step involving the turnouts is also where you want to evaluate the use of easements with the curves included in your plan as discussed earlier. It is much easier to decide on easements and install them if you don't have the scenery, etc. to have to try to fit the track layout around. The scenery including various buildings to a point should be made to fit the track layout and turnouts instead of the track layout trying to fit around the secondary areas of the system, i.e. trees, minor buildings, etc.

Step 3

Once you think your rough layout is arranged properly, mentally think through running the layout imagining what is happening as the train runs around the track you have laid out. Remember your layout should still be "loose" and not secured to the benchwork so you can make changes easily while asking yourself some of these questions about your layout and the train running to see if you have thought of all the important details involved for success.

You will save yourself a lot of time in the long run if you run imaginary trains through the unsecured layout making changes as the needs become apparent before the track is nailed to the benchwork. However, if you are just running a single train on a basic track layout with only 1-2 levels, then the majority of this step can be skipped. Otherwise...

- Thinking of the curves – are they gradual with appropriate easement, or too tight and needing easements to keep the train from jerking around the curve? Do you have more curves and necessary easements than you have room for in order to keep them far enough apart to run the trains smoothly?

- Considering the areas where the tracks cross over each other and/or the turnouts – do you have enough room for trains to pass each other without touching? Is the height of any tunnels or bridges high enough to accommodate trains adequately in terms of clearance?

- Are your turnaround areas configured to avoid any blind spots? Will the switches send the trains in the various directions they are supposed to when thrown? Are they set in big enough loops to allow the back of the train to clear before the front of the train is run back on the tracks in the opposite direction?

- Take your imaginary train through the runabouts you have planned, whether they dead-end or can reverse back to the mainline, in order to make sure the runaround track is long enough for whatever reason you need it for. It doesn't do any good to have a runaround or turnout installed if it isn't long enough to pull the entire train off the main track in order for another train to pass.

- Have you left enough room in your layout to accommodate the buildings and scenery you want as a part of your system? Are the turnout or runaround sections connected to the various industries and services as long as they need to be to have room to accomplish their purposes?

- If your various buildings are designed for usage and not just decoration, you need to make sure that their purpose can be accomplished without blocking the main line. For example, is the turn-out for the passenger train depot long enough to pull the entire passenger train off the main tracks in order for the passengers to have time to be unloaded without causing a traffic jam of trains at the depot station?

Step 4

If you are planning for more than one level, you need to determine how you are going to configure the tracks to allow trains to traverse up and down between levels. Of course you wouldn't need to figure that out if you prefer your different levels to be self-contained without any vertical movement of the trains on the various levels.

This in essence means each level is a completely separate railroad system not interconnected to any levels above or below and trains would have to be picked up and physically moved from one level to the other if desired. But assuming you have more than one level because you want your entire system to be interconnected with the ability to travel between levels, you need to plan how you are going to create layout sections that will allow that.

There are two different basic ways that will allow the trains to run throughout the various levels by following the track layout options available – you can either use helix track sections or gradual incline tract sections between levels. Both methods of movement between levels can be reversed using switches and turnarounds in order to move back to lower levels.

A helix is circular section of track that resembles a corkscrew and is quite often disguised by tunnels or trees, etc. A train run onto a helix in order to reach the next level simply follows the track line of the helix around and around until it goes up to the next level similar to how a spiral staircase works in a regular building in order to travel to and from various levels within the building.

Gradual inclines are usually fully visible with a dual purpose of adding decorative dimensions that up the visual appeal while also serving to get trains from one level to the next. Generally the elevations of these grades are gradually increased between 1% and 4%. Any sharper grades will increase the possibility that your train may not be powerful enough to climb the grade to the next level. There are several simple formulas to use when calculating the graded inclines according to specific measurements unique to your system. The formula you choose will be determined by what calculations you already know in order to determine the specifics of what you don't know in regards to gradual inclines.

- In order to figure out how many inches of track you need for your grade (or the length), determine the height measurement from the first level to the next level and divide that height by the percentage of grade you have room for which will result in how many inches of track you need to lay for that grade. For example, if the vertical distance between the 2 levels is 5 inches, and you want to create a grade with the steepest incline recommended which is 4%, divide 5 inches by 4% (or 5 divided by .04) which equals to 500 inches of track necessary to create a 4% grade in order to travel the 5 inch height between levels.

- To figure out the height that your lay-out can accommodate between levels, multiply the percentage of grade chosen (between 1% and 4%) by the length of track you have to use. Say you have 200 inches of track to use at a 4% incline. Multiply the .04 incline by the 200 inches of track which results in the finding that your second level can be up to 8 inches higher than your first level.

- Or to figure out how steep your grade percentage needs to be for the plans you have in mind, divide the height between levels with the length of tracks you have designated for the grade. To illustrate, suppose you want to run your trains between levels that have a vertical distance of 6 inches separating them and have 300 inches of track in order to do so. Divide the 6 inches of height by the 300 inches of length and you will find that your grade should be around 2%.

Creating a layout to accommodate running trains between levels doesn't necessarily have to be done at this point in the building process if figuring out where and how to do so is making things more complicated than you would prefer as a novice model railroader.

While it would be easier to include the construction of grades or helixes now before your system is attached to the benchwork, it can be done later on down the road which might take a little extra effort then but a tradeoff you might be willing to make in order to simplify the process now.

Step 5

Once your basic layout has been set, you need to lay down the roadbed across the surface of the benchwork underneath the track layout that should be loosely sitting on the surface in the desired configuration. The roadbed is simply a recreation of the ground that a real railroad would use for laying the train tracks.

Model railroaders usually create a roadbed using corkboard or foam sections that can be found in craft stores cut to fit various scale sizes most often in sections around 36 inches long that are made to be able to split down the middle to create 2 long strips.

Laying and securing the roadbed should be done a section at a time once you are confident each section is configured properly to fit your plans and space. Following these steps one section of your railroad system at a time will have your roadbed foundation finished in no time.

- Choose the first section of your surface and layout plan to start with. It is usually best to start laying the roadbed in one of the corners of the surface and it will automatically line up straight on at least two sides.

- Take a felt pen or ultra-fine tip marker to mark small dots between the track ties of the rails laid out which allows you to then move the track out of the way in order to glue down the roadbed strips following the dots you marked.

- The strips of roadbed are designed to be split in two in order to lay them flush against the dots you marked and also have the outer edges clearly marked which causes the inner edges to be obvious when split. The inner edge of each strip is lined up with the dots marked on the base surface running down the center of the tracks for the sections you are working with. Glue down 1-2 small sections of roadbed within the section of track layout you are working with then set that section of tracks back in place on top of the roadbed and go on to the next section without securing the tracks themselves yet.

- Follow this process repeatedly one section at a time until the roadbed has been glued down for the entire system.

Step 6

Next is a similar pattern of connecting sections of the actual tracks themselves that are already sitting in place on top of the roadbed in each section. Most tracks are designed to snap together with rail joiners that usually come packaged with the tracks you purchased.

Take care to make sure that each section connects to the next one smoothly by running your finger across the connection – if anything "snagged" your finger when you ran it across the connecting areas then you know it has not been sufficiently connected and you need to fix it before moving on to the next section.

Advanced model railroaders will usually solder the joints together in order to make sure the connection is a good one that is going to stay in place as it is designed to.

Step 7

After you have gone through the entire layout connecting tracks one section at a time, you then need to go back to the beginning again for round 3 of laying the tracks which involves gluing the securely connected tracks to the roadbed underneath them. The easiest and least expensive way to do so requires only 4 items: Elmer's glue, water, rubbing alcohol, and a medicine-like dropper.

Make your own glue mixture by diluting 4 parts of Elmer's glue with one part of water then add a small amount of rubbing alcohol to the mixture. The alcohol makes the glue smoother and easier to spread out the way needed.

Spreading out the glue under the tracks works best using a dropper to drop small amounts of the glue mixture between the tract ties as they are laid out. The glue will slowly spread for a little while before it hardens and dries the track into place and connects it to the roadbed.

This type of glue mixture is the most forgiving as it is transparent once dry. It is also easy to clean off any drops that get on top of the rails that would negatively influence how the trains are able to travel on the tracks.

In worst-case scenario, if spots of dried glue are ignored without being cleaned off the rails it could cause a derailment as the trains wheels won't be able to keep a connection with the rails as needed if there are significant amounts of dried glue stuck on top of the tracks. You also need to be very careful with the glue used around the turnout sections of tracks as glue accidentally winding up in the switch mechanisms can cause them to not work correctly if they even work at all.

How To Run Wires

As with anything else in model railroading, you have several options for wiring your train to run by electricity that can be as simple or as complex as you prefer. Whichever method you choose to start with must be done right in order for your train to run properly. Those new to model railroading might prefer to start with the easiest wiring set-up initially as it can always be upgraded or expanded further down the road after you have gained some confidence in running your trains in general.

When deciding on your wiring scheme, there are 6 basic scenarios to choose from.

- **Single Train Control** – This is the basic wiring plan that you start with as the foundation to your wiring plans where additional component are added as needed or wanted either at the same time or at a later date. Through a powerpack (or central control box), this wiring system will control a single train running on a single set or level of tracks. Your railroad can run with this control as long as you need until ready to take on the challenge of adding additional wiring elements and choices.

- **Blocks** – Now add in the blocks. Blocks are sections of train track that can be isolated electrically from the mainline and mainly used to park locomotives that aren't needed at the moment but must be stored somewhere that won't block the mainline.

- **Complex System** – Four or more blocks on mainline coupled with two powerpacks is a more complex wiring plan that requires installation of at least 4 different blocks throughout your system and needs to be run with two powerpack controls.

- **Cab Control** – Cab control must have the blocks and powerpacks (just referred to in #3 above) to in order to gain the ability to run two different locomotives as desired on a single train track. Since these trains will run independently of each other meaning one can't decide what the other is going to do, you must be closely involved in running the trains and watching where they are going because head-on collisions, etc. are possible if you don't keep the trains supervised and moved out of the way as needed to prevent accidents or derailments.

- **Digital Command Control (DCC)** – A digital command system is great fun to use with a model railroad system if you are comfortable with digital technology. The DCC control box is the "brain" of the train system where each locomotive has a different receiver connected to specified engines. Since the receiver inside each locomotive "talks" to the DCC, you can control all the functions available for your trains electronically with just one set of wires. The receiver/responder is different for each locomotive and allows a unique identity to be given to each engine.

- **DCC linked to computer** – Since we do live in such a technologically advanced age, it is no surprise that the DCC can be connected to a computer allowing ultimate control to be exercised through the computer and not just the control box. Being able to connect and control your system through your computer opens up even more ways to enjoy an "old-fashioned" hobby with modern technology.

If you are somewhat comfortable with digital technology, the most useful wiring layout is probably the DCC option from the start as it will cut down the time for installing the wiring both now and when you want to upgrade the electronics later. The necessity for needing only one set of wires installed to run multiple trains is a possibility you might not want to overlook. This decision will most likely be based on how comfortable you are with electronic technology.

If you are building the system for yourself or others who might not be comfortable or familiar with the technological advances we have seen become available in the last few decades, then you might need to make the wiring as simple as possible and involves the least amount of technology if it is more frustrating to learn technology than is preferred in any given scenario. And just because you install the wiring technology, it doesn't mean you have to use it until you are ready to do so.

Wiring is usually the most complicated part of your railroad as a whole and the options above only cover a portion of the detailed information you will need in order to personalize the model railroad to fit your layout plans. There are extensive aspects of what can and can't be done with wiring which those who are familiar with electrical systems might find as one of the more enjoyable parts of building a model railroad.

Where to Find Layout Ideas

Layout ideas for model railroads are pretty much endless because any plan can be "quirked" to your preferences or you can create your own plan from scratch if desired. Regardless, unless you specifically set out to duplicate a real railroad, your system will be as unique as you are. Just as there is no one else nor will there ever be anyone else just like you, so too are the thoughts, preferences, and adjustments for the model railroad created first in your mind and then transferred to 3-D in real life.

That being said, the website http://www.freetrackplans.com, offers many different (& free!) trackplan layouts that you can either browse through and choose one that meets your fancy, or you can look through them all just for inspiration for designing own unique layout from scratch – also known as "scratch work".

Not only does this site offer various plans, it also has them categorized into sizes that would fit whatever benchwork space you have. For example, the surface space for your own railroad might be 4 feet by 4 feet and you can look at different 4x4 layout plans with various themes that they have available. They also offer layout plans for scaled versions of some of the more popular real railroad systems if you prefer your railroad to model a specific railroad in reality.

The sources for track ideas and layout plans are many and varied, both free and for purchase as well. Quite a few railroad enthusiasts enjoy sharing the love of railroading and tips to improve them simply for fun and are often available for specific questions you might have whether online, in person, or over the phone.

There are also sources that will fully customize and illustrate the layout plan that you envision and either cannot translate it to paper plans yourself or would rather just pay someone else to do so from your ideas and preferences.

If you are more comfortable gathering information offline, public libraries across the country usually have a good supply of model railroad books available for checkout or as reference books only to be used within the library. There are also quite a few magazine subscriptions available for model railroaders that are a great source for all kinds of information about model railroading including layout plans.

Chapter 5: Buying Locomotives

The very heart and soul of any model railroad are the trains that run on it. All of the planning and building you complete is directly or indirectly focused on running and showcasing the trains. So if you are going to "splurge" with any railroad item purchase it should be on quality locomotives and/or rolling stock to a lesser extent.

It is important to consider the many options available and their pros and cons in terms of your layout and preferences. Not only is this important for the aesthetic value, purchasing the right locomotives is vital to the successful enjoyment of your railroad with the least frustrating complications as possible.

It is worth spending the money on high quality locomotives to insure the successful operation of the train through every section of your model no matter how it's configured. In general, low-cost is equal to inferior quality for most locomotives and the old adage "you get what you pay for" is certainly relevant here.

Investing in well-built, sturdy locomotives in the beginning is sure to save much frustration down the road when you discover the cheap engine is unable to generate enough power to climb grades or pull long trains.

Railroaders who use the cheap locomotives that come in many model kits find it hard to get the locomotives moving and have to utilize frequent "push starts" in order to give the engine the momentum it needs in order to take off from a stationary point.

But that process is also problematic because frequently the inferior locomotives are building momentum when being pushed that allows them to take off suddenly and unexpectedly causing them to go straight into derailment as the train to flies right off the tracks. If this happens too many times, you may just lose all the enjoyment and pleasure a model railroad has to offer.

How to Select the Right Locomotives

There are a few locomotives details you need to note in order to choose the best locomotives for your system. Whether you are purchasing single engines to upgrade the ones you already have, or deciding which railroad scale you want to use, some aspects are important to consider no matter which scale you are interested in using.

- **Scale** – It probably goes without saying, but if not…you first need to make sure whatever locomotives you are considering for purchase are the same scale size as the rest of your system. Locomotives must match the scale in order to work in the system but in the excitement of searching for just the right one, scale-size might be overlooked. It isn't easy to make this silly mistake but if you happen to do so (after all, even railroaders are human and capable of foolish errors!), it will prove to be a self-caused but aggravating mistake that can be avoided.

- **Metal Wheels & Gears** – The best locomotives are ones with an abundance of metal wheels connected to an abundance of gears in order to create a smoothly running train.

- **Metal Frame** – A quality locomotive will have a heavy metal frame that is sturdy and difficult to break. Plastic-framed locomotives are usually inferior and won't stand up to very many accidents or derailments and will only be able to hit the floor a few times before being broken beyond repair.

- **Weight** – The weight of a locomotive is also important because lighter-weight engines will tend to derail easier. Not only do you want to use metal frames in order to prevent or lessen the risk of derailment accidents, metal frames are also heavier and the weight of the locomotive is an important factor in terms of power and strength needed to pull a train. Heavier engines will keep principles of physics and gravity in good working order as a heavier engine is able to build and retain forward motion better. The weight of the locomotive is one of the most important deciding factors in whether or not your train can gain enough speed before hitting an incline and making it to the top of the hill.

- **Flywheels** – You also want to purchase a locomotive that has solid metal flywheels. The flywheels are basically cylinders that are connected in line with the motor. These are used to slow down the initial take off power of the motor in order for it to smoothly start building up speed without sudden, jerky movement in taking off that motors will cause if flywheels are not attached. Flywheels also smooth out the motion experienced when stopping a train so that it doesn't come to a halt in a neck-snapping stop.

- **Inclines & Downgrades** – It is also important to consider your layout when choosing a locomotive to run it. Quality of the locomotive is slightly less important if you do not have any significant inclines that your train will need more power in order to travel up an incline or the power needed to slow your train when it is heading downhill so that it doesn't pick up too much speed causing a derailment at the bottom or on a curve in the middle of the downgrade. The percentage of incline is a factor at this point also. Remember inclines need to be between 1% and 4% and the smaller the incline percentage, the less power it will require to reach the top.

Things to Consider When Buying Locomotives

In addition to the technical details necessary to consider when buying locomotives, there are a few things to consider other than those details listed above that are important to consider in order to build the best model railroad you can with your own unique preferences and tastes.

- **Future Goals** – Purchasing locomotives is a little different from purchasing other parts of the system. Basically you are looking at a significant investment when you purchase a quality engine that necessitates your choice to be as versatile as possible. This is for both the railroad you have now as well as the railroad you might want to upgrade it to later on down the road.

  While you can employ the principle of "buy now and upgrade later" (that is reasonable for most of the other parts of your system) if you want to, it is more efficient and less expensive in the long run to purchase top of the line locomotives from the beginning if you can afford to do so. It is better to have more powerful engines than your current system requires than to have engines that are only strong enough now but will be too weak to work with any expansions of your railroad in the future.

- **New or Used** – We have a great tool available to use when enjoying the model-railroading hobby that our ancestors did not have for the most part – thrift stores and other sources for purchasing used products.

These days you can usually purchase just about anything you are looking for in used condition for a lower price. But choosing whether to buy new or used isn't just about how much it costs but is also better for the environment by recycling someone else's quality locomotives when acquiring used before they wind up in a dump or trash heap somewhere because the original owner purchased new locomotives. Buying used also makes sense if you are new to railroading and experimenting to see if it is a hobby you will enjoy for years to come or not.

- **Sources** – Depending on what foundational system you are using, there are many sources to look to in order to find the best deals for purchasing locomotives that will work for your system. You can be certain that you will be able to find great quality engines to buy from just about any commercial toy or hobby store but those might not always be the best choice in terms of cost.

Many auction websites like eBay are a great place to start looking for a locomotive bargains whether purchasing new or used. Individuals and commercial stores both will post railroad items for sale online and you can eventually find the perfect bargain if you have the time to look for it and the patience to wait for a good deal to pop up.

Most of those same toy and hobby stores you can visit in person will also have an online store where they tend to advertise clearance items, coupons, or short-term sales that might not be available when visiting the store in person or vice versa.

Whether purchasing new or used, there are always bargains to be found if you look for them long enough. But be sure to search for bargains with a healthy dose of skepticism and caution in order to limit vulnerability to scams and possible "lemon" items offered for purchase. If you are not familiar with and confident in the seller's credentials, consider the possibility that any price that seems too cheap may have quality issues that are undisclosed which might just illustrate the principle of "too good to be true".

Purchasing/Building Your Rolling Stock

Rolling stock is a term that applies to various railroad cars that are designed to attach to a locomotive. The use of the word "car" might be confusing to railroad newbie's because we generally tend to think "cars" refer to automobiles. But in terms of trains and railroads, cars are just another name for rolling stock that locomotives pull. They include passenger cars, chemical or liquid tankers, stock cars for transporting animals, freight cars for the transport of goods, etc. In general, most railroad cars fit into 6 basic types: passenger, tank, box, spine, coiled steel, and flat.

- **Passenger Cars** – Rather self-explanatory, passenger cars are created and maintained for the sole purpose of transporting people and their luggage when traveling.

- **Tank Cars** – These cars are designed for transporting liquids and are usually the cars that hit the news circuit with any derailment or accident because they are often carrying extremely toxic chemicals that are dangerous and potentially lethal if spilled. They are most often used for transporting various liquid chemicals but some also transport milk for human consumption or various gasses like liquid petroleum, propane, etc.

- **Box Cars** – One of the most commonly seen railroad cars are the box cars used to transport freight and various dry goods both edible and non-edible such as crates of preserved food items (canned, processed, etc.), commercial dry goods, automobile parts and tires, etc. These cars are also familiar for their reputation of unofficial transport of "hobos" – people that are generally homeless and decide to travel around the country by sneaking into boxcars and hiding out until they choose a location to get off the train.

- **Spine Cars** – This type of car is rolling stock (rather redundantly named) usually used to carry rolling trailers that are made for semi-trucks to pull cross-country in order to transport freight over the various interstates and highways.

- **Coiled Steel Cars** – These cars are usually covered because they are used to transport gigantic coils of thickly gauged steel wiring and the like. They need to be covered in order to protect the contents from getting wet and rusty if traveling through rainy weather.

- **Flat Cars** – Flat cars are also commonly seen similar to the familiar box cars because they are also frequently used in transporting vehicles of many kinds including cars, boats, multi-purpose trailers, farm equipment, and military vehicles like tanks, jeeps, and humvees, etc.

No matter what type of railroad cars you are considering for purchase, some aspects of the cars need to be thoughtfully considered in order to make sure you are buying quality cars that will work as you need or expect them to.

- **Wheels** – How well the wheels work on railroad cars is a very important detail affecting both quality as well as enjoyment of your railroad system. It is helpful if you are able to handle any cars you might want to purchase with your hands in order to physically check and feel some of the more important details.

You need to check to see how long a wheel will turn smoothly if given a push with your hand. If the wheel(s) only turns once before stopping you have a great clue as to the quality of the car and just how smooth (or not) it will run on your train tracks.

Ideally, the wheels should continue to run even as they slow after a manual shove in any direction. They should not run one cycle around and stop. You also want to make sure that the wheels don't wobble. Wobbling wheels significantly increase the chances for train derailments directly caused by said wobbly wheels.

- **Plastic or Metal** – Railroad cars don't necessarily need the heavier weight that works better for locomotives because they will be carrying freight that adds to their weight, and directed by the heavy locomotives at the front of the train. However, while the car form itself can be made of plastic or metal, the axle for the car needs to be metal in order to be strong enough to carry heavy freight without buckling.

- **Wheel Distance** – You also need to check out the distance between the wheels connected to the axle. They have to have the same equal distance apart in order to run properly and this is one train element that might just be better if made out of plastic instead of metal because plastic wheels are more often made to be adjustable in order to allow a custom fit to the tracks perfectly resulting in a smoothly running train.

Chapter 6: Constructing Scenery

The scenery your model train runs through and the structures included in the scenery ("scenery" is understood to include structures) are one of the most enjoyable aspects of railroading. The scenery of whatever model railroad you observed prior to building your own is most likely one of the main details that caught your attention in the first place.

The panoramic layout is a component with arguably the greatest value in customizing your railroad in whatever direction suits your own personal tastes. It might also be the most enjoyable step as whole during the construction process as the sky's the limit when determining what overall look you want your model railroad to portray.

Scenery choices can play a big role in gaining the admiration of family and friends and carry high potential in attracting enough interest to give you chances to infect others with a love for model railroads as you show off the system you produced through your own efforts (can fun labor be described as "hard work"?).

Some basic layout and scenery options have been mentioned previously but there are more details to learn that will further empower your imagination and creative juices while also giving you the information you need in order to plan your own unique railroad. Here are some of the important things to consider when choosing and building your system.

Labor & Finances Involved

One of the many good things about choosing model railroads as a hobby is that you always have options available while determining what steps to take in building the scenery. There are different ways to accomplish the final result and the methods you choose depend largely on your own personal preferences as well as the finances available.

Whether you have a small budget for creating scenery for your railroad or can afford whatever you want, there are wide arrays of options that vary according to cost and labor preferences in achieving the overall mood you want your railroad to portray in terms of scenery.

- **Pre-Fabricated** – There are many model railroad kits available for purchase that contain everything you need including the scenery, or you can also purchase accessory kits that contain only scenery items for the railroad. These pre-fabricated scenery layouts come in a wide range of price points that will fit any budget – you can find scenery sets that cost less than $50 as a minimum all the way up to scenery layouts that can cost thousands of dollars. This is the easiest and fastest way to create the scenery for your railroad and they usually have layout diagrams included to make it even easier.

- **Piece-by-Piece** – It can be much more rewarding to build your own scenery layout a piece at a time which allows for personalizing each choice to fit your dream railroad. The same sources you went to in order to purchase your train set will almost always carry scenic items that sell individually.

The scale differences are not nearly as important as they are with other railroad pieces that require the same-scaled components in order for the train to run successfully. You aren't usually as limited in your scenery choices by scale size as they have little to do with fitting to the actual mechanics of the running train, but the structures in your scenery should complement the scale of the train set you are operating. Scale sizes serve to broaden your choices while building a mix-n-match scenery layout. For example, you can use trees sized differently from several scales in order to create a more visually attractive, complex, and artistic mountain, orchard, or park, etc.

- **Self-Crafted Scenery** – You can also go a step further in adding the personal touch to your scenic layout by creating the pieces yourself with various crafting techniques. While some railroaders have no interest in using their own hand labor to build the scenery, others find this one of the most satisfying parts of building the system in general.

There are many step-by-step instructions available online and in books and magazines as well that will allow even those who are the most "challenged" with understanding craft techniques to successfully produce the scenery layout they have envisioned for their train system.

Making your scenery yourself allows for the ultimate experience in imagination as well as personalization. While doing it yourself is more labor intensive, craft supplies for making your own pieces are often cheaper than buying the ready-made product and also have many more options available for choosing your own colors, etc.

Overall Theme

When planning your model railroad scenery and layout, you need to choose an overall theme or "look" you want your completed railroad to portray. Some railroad enthusiasts want to create a strict replication of real railroads from the past or present while others enjoy combining detailed parts of a real railroad with unique and imaginative details of their own that may or may not be realistic. A few things to consider when choosing a theme for your railroad are:

- **Perfection vs. Imperfection** – Personal preference will dictate just how "perfect" and clean your railroad theme is. While being neither right nor wrong, some will enjoy creating as perfect a model train display as possible with as few flaws as possible. They enjoy a neat and clean overall appearance with the scenery that creates the perception of being well maintained with none of the imperfections that come with real life.

  On the flip side, other railroaders prefer to create a scenic layout for their system that is as realistic as possible including flaws that are often seen in real railroading scenarios. For example, suppose your overall theme is an industrial railroad portraying a scene where trains are working with heavy industry needs such as chemical transportation, coal delivery, freight shipments, etc.

  If you want to achieve a more realistic mood, add some imperfect details such as graffiti, dirty or wrecked railroad cars in the staging yard, weeds growing around the tracks or the base of buildings, individual pieces of trash blown around in the wind and caught against a fence line, scratched up and rusty equipment, a small, abandoned storage shed with the roof caving in, etc. Anything commonly found in an industrial setting can be replicated for a more realistic touch to your system.

But if you prefer your railroad to be as aesthetically perfect as possible, those things will never be seen. Your locomotives will always look clean, there will be no weeds around anywhere, cars will be gleaming white or other colors without a scratch or spec of dirt, all buildings small and large will look well-kept with no visual problems, there will be no graffiti to be found, etc. This look will be less realistic, but more enjoyable to those who enjoy a neat and orderly layout that is as attractive and clean as possible.

- **Location** – Choosing a general location to model can be helpful in giving your imagination a starting point if nothing else. Sometimes it is hard to decide what look you want to achieve if you don't begin without observing the details of a railroad that exists presently in real life.

A helpful choice with this step is that you do not have to necessarily see the railroad you are considering in person because pictures of real railroad locations are readily found online or in libraries and can help guide your imaginative ideas. These real locations to observe for the purpose of sparking your own imagination don't necessarily have to contain commercial areas.

For example, consider the scenic location of the Wild West in the early days of building and operating the first cross-country rail line mentioned in the beginning of this book. You can consider a city location along the line, a mountainous area it traveled through, a canyon scene that was known for ambush by Indians or robbers, etc., or even the location exhibits at the front of the line while laying the first train tracks through the area.

You may prefer a scenery layout that has no buildings included or perhaps just a couple. Take the scenery just mentioned in the general location the Wild West days. If you choose a layout to consider that looks like the areas commonly known for ambush, you might not have any buildings at all or perhaps just a tiny cabin in the distance or an abandoned Trading Store beside the rails. This choice would cause the focus to be placed on the train itself and the landscape it is running through complete with wild animals and everything else seen while running a train through the countryside.

Choosing a scenic theme is necessary if you want your railroad to present an organized and cohesive look overall. For this section, the point is not necessarily creating a realistic theme but rather the point is focused on the overall look achieved for whatever theme you choose.

Seasonal Touches

Another fun part of model railroading is the ability to change or add to the scenery according to the season and/or holidays if you choose to. You can add "snow" for the winter, Christmas lights in December, Halloween decorative touches, or even personalized temporary additions for important days within your home and family such as birthdays, graduations, weddings, new babies, romantic messages, etc. There really is no end to the enjoyment you can find playing with model scenery in ways that are also socially rewarding.

Scenery Materials

Creating the scenic vision for your railroad can be mentally stimulating in a good way as you try to recreate tiny versions of different aspects that are a little challenging to duplicate on a smaller level. The smallest scaled trains need realistic details as much as the larger recreations do but it is more difficult to scale down some of the specific details.

If you put enough thought and/or research into it, you will find there is always some way to create the minute details you need. For example, think of what the ground looks like under and around real railroad tracks. Usually you can see gravel around the tracks. But creating the tiniest scaled version of gravel might not be so easy unless you take the time to brainstorm what might or might not work. Eventually, you may come to the realization that crushed nutmeats of various types have a good scaled down resemblance to real gravel with variations in size and color just like the real thing.

Maybe you want to add snow to your scenery temporarily. There are many materials available to accomplish that resulting in a realistic snow-scape. Spun-glass called "angel's hair", Styrofoam peanuts, sand, salt, and quilting batting are a few of the options you can choose from depending on the look you are trying to achieve, how long you want to keep it as a part of the scenery, and what it will take to remove it when desired.

Overall, your scenery and structure layout can be as simple or as complicated as you prefer and allows for remodeling as often as you want. Scenery details are exciting for those with an artistic bent and much enjoyment can be found in recreating small-scale scenery that builds the railroad image you have developed in your imagination. Scenic details can also make your model railroad a treasure to pass down the line to future generations who can upgrade or restore the railroad you left behind and a way to keep your memory alive to your future descendants.

Conclusion

In a complex and ever changing-world, it can be hard to find hobbies that are able to be enjoyed by several different generations of people all at the same time and model railroading offers that valuable possibility. Some of the most valuable gifts we have to share are those of simple enjoyment between family and friends while playing with a family-friendly hobby that is fun for all ages and genders. Regardless of the reasons why you are looking into building your own model railroad, it is a versatile entertainment choice that is able to fit anyone's lifestyle, available space, and finances.

Model Railroads & Lifestyle

There are sizes and themes for various railroad models that can fit into you own unique way of life and natural rhythm for your family adding entertainment and memories that will last a lifetime. Building a model railroad can be enjoyable no matter what stage of life you might be in...from a small railroad setup on the countertop of your studio apartment, to the railroad you begin building with your significant other while dating that goes along for the ride when you marry and begin a life together.

As children start to come along you may not have the time for much involvement with your model, but it can become a sporadic activity whenever needed for relaxation or to "get away" when children are too small to be involved. Later the model can become a fun hobby to enjoy with your children.

As the years go by, your family situation might develop into a lifestyle that includes the addition of grandparents as permanent family members within the household. That might be a challenging transition time where model railroading endeavors can help strengthen the bonds between generations along with respect for areas that different generations excel at.

Eventually your lifestyle may come full circle as a senior citizen living independently again. Having the familiar railroading hobby as part of your new lifestyle can add a level of security and safety while still being a mentally stimulating activity when you try to figure out how to include technological advances in your system while maintaining the integrity of the overall railroad theme you want to portray.

Model Railroads & Space Availability

Another well-known valuable characteristic of model railroads is the choices available in terms of size and scale that make the hobby accessible to anyone no matter how little space they have to dedicate to it. The tiniest scaled versions are small enough to fit on a nightstand while the larger scales are big enough to ride on personally and can be a lot of fun to build outside for family and friends to enjoy train rides throughout your extensive property.

Whether you live in a one-room studio apartment or enjoy sharing a mansion and many acres of land with your loved ones, there are always railroad options that can fit the space you have.

Model Railroads & Finances

If you are unfamiliar with model railroading and how much or little it can cost, you might think that you do not have the money to "waste" with this hobby. But it may be a pleasant surprise as you begin researching your options for building a railroad. You will find that the hobby can fit into anyone's budget. It is a great way to spend that "fun money" that is usually a part of anyone's finances even if the amount is no more than what it would cost to see a movie once a week, or indulge in cappuccino 3 days a week before work, etc.

While it may take longer to accomplish building a completed model railroad a little at a time whenever you have a few extra dollars that can be reasonably spent on hobbies or indulgences, it can be done and might just be more rewarding than if you have large amounts of money to spend on the hobby whenever you choose.

There can be great satisfaction building a railroad even when finances are tight because you will find that you are more creative than you realize. Even if you don't necessarily have financial limitations, you might find it both personally challenging and even a teaching tool of sorts if you have children involved to set a budget for your railroad endeavor and stick to it even after you have completed the layout plans and know what you have envisioned for your own unique railroad.

Whether you build your railroad piece-by-piece or as a completed set, you can start with creating your plan on paper without costing a penny at first. Then you can begin to assemble it as you have the money to do so. If you prefer to purchase model train sets you can start with inexpensive models under $50 which can be reasonably saved up over a comparatively short amount of time.

Of course it goes without saying when your finances are not an issue to be concerned with you can afford to buy intricate and expensive train sets but that doesn't necessarily mean they would be more personally enjoyable than the set you gathered and built slowly as the money and materials became available.

Glossary

AAR — Association of American Railroads.

AC (alternating current) — Electric current that can go in different directions back and forth through a wire.

Access Area – An opening in the middle of a benchwork layout that allows for access within arms' length to any spot of the model layout.

Accessories — Anything of the model other than locomotives, cars, and tracks. Includes switches, lighting, small motors for animation, etc.

Articulated — A locomotive where the engine moves unconnected from the frame.

Auto Carrier — A railroad car designed to carry automobiles and other vehicles.

Baggage Car — A car for passenger's baggage or sometimes freight shipments in passenger trains.

Ballast — Building material under railroad tracks for the drainage of water while giving a cushion of sorts for the track.

Benchwork — The structure which holds up the roadbed where the track and scenery of a layout is installed.

Block — Sections of track that are able to be separated electrically from the rest of the wiring whenever needed.

Box Car — An enclosed railroad car that protects its contents from outside environmental factors.

Branch — A short section of track that allows trains to move off the mainline in order to provide service to an industry or business, etc.

Bumper — Placed at the dead end of a line to stop trains from running over the edge.

Cab (electrical) — Electric equipment needed to control one train.

Cab (locomotive) — The section of the locomotive that house all the controls, etc.

Cab Control — A system that allows one of two or more cabs to be connected, one at a time, to any block of track for electricity needs.

Can Motor — A motor usually found in more expensive locomotives.

Catenary — Overhead wires for electrical locomotives.

Clearance Gauge — A tool that determines if there is enough space between rails and trains to allow for passing each other without any direct contact.

Coach — A railroad car used in a passenger train that is the least expensive way to travel on a train with chairs that remain upright but can be tilted back for relaxation reasons if desired. No sleeping quarters on coach cars.

Code (rail) — The height of a rail measured in one thousandths of an inch without the decimal point.

Command Control — A system for controlling trains that enables more than one locomotive to operate at different speeds in different directions. DCC is the most common command control system.

Container — A boxcar type without wheels that has constant measurements and is used for freight transport when the boxes will be moved from ships to trains. Most of these containers are designed to be carried by rail, truck, and water (ships).

Couplers — The hardware used to join the different cars and locomotives in a train.

Craftsman Kit — A kit which includes all of the materials needed to build a structure or railroad car using highly detailed and intricate instructions.

Crossover — Two turnouts running parallel that will allow a train to go from one track to the other.

DCC (Digital Command Control) — the NMRA sponsored command control system that follows their standard in order for equipment produced by different manufacturers to be operated together.

Easement — A curve of slowing radius placed before a curve in order to "ease" a train into the curve gradually creating a railroad that looks more attractive when running while avoiding the jerking activity resulting from curves that are too sharp.

Engineer — The "driver" of train locomotives.

Express Car — A railroad boxcar assigned to express postal shipping.

Fine Scale — A scale that does not have exact measurements like the other scales. Instead it is used as a method to create tighter layouts that carry more subjective personal appeal.

Flat Car — A freight car with a load deck about the same size as the entire car in order to allow for bigger item shipment.

Flextrack — A 3 foot long section of track that can be straight or will flex into curved if wanted.

Flywheel — A round metal weight connected to the drive shaft of a motor to help smooth out start-ups and stops.

FRA (Federal Railroad Administration) — A federal government railroad regulatory agency in use now.

FRED (Flashing Rear End Device) — Small mechanical equipment attached to the last car that flashes bright red at the end of the train in place of a caboose.

Freight Car — Railroad cars designed to carry freight of any kind.

Freight Yard — Track sections on a layout used for switching freight cars and creating customized trains.

Frog — The spot on the track layout where its rails cross the turnout's rails in a switch.

G Gauge — A size variation of model trains on rails that are 64 mm (2.519") apart.

Gauge — The distance between the rails of train tracks.

Grab Iron (Grab) — Handles on the sides of cars or equipment.

Grade — Section of tracks allow the train to transverse between higher and lower levels.

Guard Rail (Bridge) — Rails laid on the tracks over a bridge in order to avoid derailments.

Handlaid Track — A railroad term used in model railroader to describe sections of track that the railroader created and laid himself.

Helix — A of track similar to the circular staircases found in houses and is used as a transportation tool to get trains up and down to different levels of the layout.

Helper — Extra locomotives added to a train when more power is needed to operate a train.

HO Scale — A model train replica ratio that is 1:87 as compared to full-size trains.

Hopper Car — A railroad car built to allow unloading from the bottom of the side walls used to transports various grains, and grain-like freight.

Hostler — The name for a rail worker that moves trains and cars around as needed from various trains or other locations.

Junction — A place where 2 or more railway routes either merge together or diverge to separate routes. This allows trains to transfer from one route to another. Train traffic is controlled by turnouts (switches) and signals.

Kitbash — Altering the parts of a kit to produce a car or structure that is unique, or combining parts from two or more kits to produce the same result.

Layout — The sum of the track, scenery, buildings, locomotives and cars of a model railroad.

Main Line — The primary route or most heavily used tracks of a railroad.

MMR — Master Model Railroader. One who has completed the requirements established by the NMRA by obtaining certificates in the Achievement Program as a "Master" of at least seven areas of model railroading.

MOW — Maintenance of way. Used to maintain the track and track structure of a railroad.

N Scale — A model train replica ratio that is 1:160 as compared to full-size trains.

Narrow Gauge — Rails spaced smaller than standard gauge that are often used in logging areas.

NMRA Gauge — A track gauge measurement set and approved by the NMRA.

NMRA — The National Model Railroad Association.

O Scale — A model train replica ratio that is 1:48 as compared to full-size trains.

OO Scale — A model train replica ratio that is 1:76 as compared to full-size trains.

Operation — Running trains on a layout ideally in a realistic manner such as the schedule of passenger trains, stock transport, etc.

Passenger Car — A railroad car designed specifically for transporting people and a small amount of their luggage, etc.

Passing Siding — Track sections that allow trains to pull over in order to allow another train to pass usually on a single-track line.

Postal Car — A railroad car created specifically for use by the United States Postal Service.

Power Pack — A fully contained electrical box commercially produced that houses the switches, wiring, and controls necessary for running a model railroad.

Prototype — An example of the real item to use when building scaled down versions of a model railroad. In technical terms of ratio, prototypes are 1:1 ratio.

Rail Joiner — A piece of metal or plastic flattened into a "C" shape to join 2 pieces of tracks while keeping them aligned.

Rail — A piece of steel shaped like a "T" in order to support various materials in order to form the tracks for railroad cars to travel on.

Ready-To-Run — Usually a term to describe rolling stock that is purchased whole with no assembly required before running on a model railroad.

Recommended Practice — Model railroad advice from the NMRA not necessarily required but highly recommended for optimal running of a model train.

Reverse Loop — A track arrangement of curved pieces that allows a train to turn around and reconnect to the mainline in the opposite direction but still on the same track.

Roadbed — In model railroading, roadbed is the material directly underneath the train system and on top of the benchwork that is used to securely attach the rail system while also adding cushioning materials, etc. where needed in order to run the train safely without undesired movement.

Rolling Stock — All of the different types of the different types of railroad cars built to run on railroad tracks to carry out a variety of purposes and transportation needs.

S Scale — A model train replica ratio that is 1:64 as compared to full-size trains.

Scale — The ratio of size of a model to the size of the real thing. A model train replica systems of ratios giving a comparison figure when looking at model railroads compared to full-size railroads.

Scenery — All the items used to create attractive model railroad layouts which included buildings and all – everything added for visual appeal excluding locomotives and railroad cars for the most part.

Scratch Build — A model piece that is constructed by the railroader from scratch by self-creating all the details that can possibly be made without commercial help.

Sectional Track — Railroad track sections generally all the same size and usually used by novice railroaders who need a simplified process for building a model railroad.

Shake-the-Box Kit — A pre-fabricated kit of various railroad elements designed for the beginner that requires minimal assembling...simply takes a "shake of the box" it comes in before it is assembled and ready to roll.

Siding — A section of tracks that branch off either or both sides of the mainline in order to remove trains from running on the main track line for whatever reason.

Signal — A mechanism similar to a traffic light for automobiles that is meant to signal the train engineer about the conditions of the railroad tracks further down the line. A red signal indicates trouble ahead, etc.

Sleeping Car — A passenger car built that also contains sleeping quarters and raises ticket prices from what is charged when traveling coach.

Solder — Metal that is designed to heat up and melt with lower temperatures in order to permanently connect metals together with a stronger bond than most other bonding agents offer.

Staging Yard — An area of a model railroad usually specifically dedicated as a parking/working lot of sorts for locomotives and railroad cars to be rearranged, repaired, or stored in multiple staging yards throughout the layout.

Standard — A measurement set and required in order to facilitate and guarantee railroad parts that are built by different manufacturers but fully interchangeable with each other.

Switch (track) — A necessary mechanical device that changes the direction of travel for nearby trains when flipped or engaged.

Tank Car — A railroad car meant for transporting various liquids such as chemicals, milk, and gasses, etc.

Terminal Block — A technical device necessary to connect the different wires needed for running a model train electronically.

Tie — The cross parts under or beside railroad tracks that connect and secure the track line into one unit.

Track — A crosswise creation of strong components laid out specifically in a way needed for locomotives and rail cars to accomplish forward travel.

Train Set — A one-unit purchase from a single manufacturer that contains all the different pieces necessary in order to build the entire railroad system advertised including tracks, locomotives, and cars, etc.

Turnout — A section of railroad tracks that are sometimes also called "switches" which causes them to be confused with the switches used in electrical systems so are also known as turnouts which is the preferred term to avoid confusion. It allows the tracks to re-direct the direction of a train whenever engaged.

Weathering — An activity named for creating artificial results or damage to objects that would naturally occur with outdoor buildings and cars exposed to environmental weather factors long term.

Wye — A section of track formed in the general shape of a "Y" that allows a train to be turned in different directions enabling it to turn around without have to be picked up and turned manually.

Yard — An designated area for unloading arriving trains, storing cars, and rearranging care for various reasons.

Z scale — A model train replica ratio that is 1:220 as compared to full-size trains.

Made in the USA
Columbia, SC
27 November 2022

72162750R00070